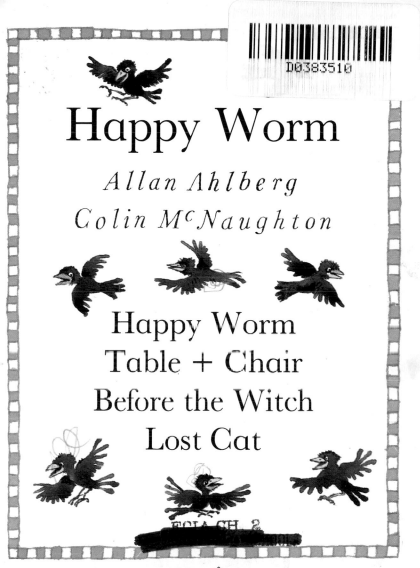

Happy Worm

Allan Ahlberg
Colin McNaughton

Happy Worm
Table + Chair
Before the Witch
Lost Cat

RANDOM HOUSE 🏠 NEW YORK

First American Edition, 1985.
Copyright © 1985 by Walker Books Ltd. All rights
reserved under International and Pan-American Copyright
Conventions. Published in the United States by Random
House, Inc., New York. Originally published in Great Britain by
Walker Books Ltd., London.

Library of Congress Cataloging in Publication Data: Ahlberg, Allan. Happy worm. (Red nose
readers) Contents: Happy worm—Table + chair—Before the witch—Lost cat. SUMMARY:
Labeled pictures introduce vocabulary and such concepts as cause and effect, opposites, and
parts of a whole. 1. Vocabulary—Juvenile literature. [1. Vocabulary]
I. McNaughton, Colin.   II. Title.   III. Series: Ahlberg, Allan. Red nose readers.
PE1449.A345   1985   428.1   84-27742
ISBN: 0-394-87196-0 (trade); 0-394-97196-5 (lib. bdg.)

Manufactured in Singapore

1 2 3 4 5 6 7 8 9 0

Happy Worm

a happy worm

a sad worm

a happy bird

a sad bird

a happy cat

a sad cat

a happy dog

a sad dog

a happy dog

Table + Chair

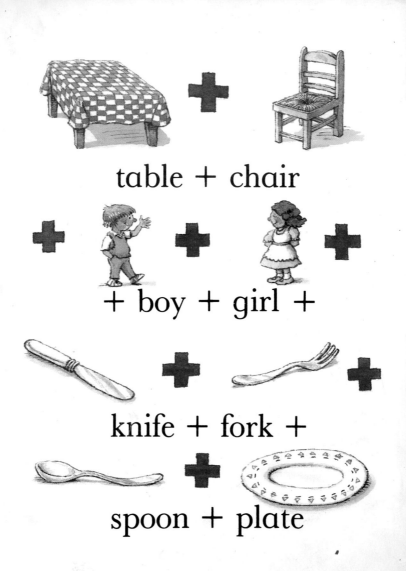

table + chair

+ boy + girl +

knife + fork +

spoon + plate

+ sandwich +

cake + Jell-O

+ drink + hat

+ popper =

party

Before the Witch

before the witch

after the witch

before the spider

after the spider

before the wolf

after the wolf

before the pie
was opened

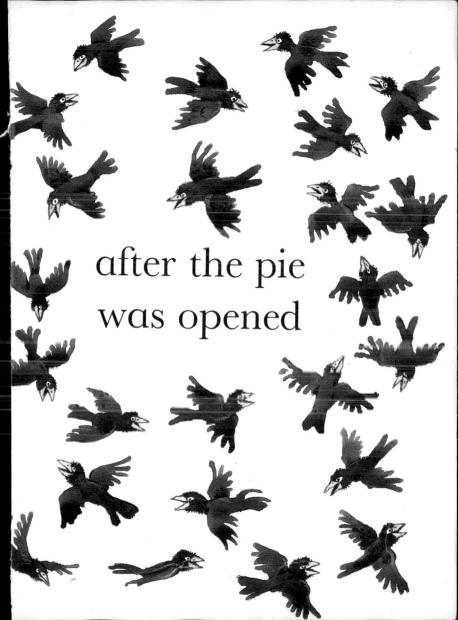

after the pie
was opened

before the kiss

after the kiss

Lost Cat

cat

no tail

no legs

no body

no whiskers

no ears

no cat